THE HAN
Bucket
List

100 Ways to Have A
Real Hanover Experience!

Ann E. Diviney

Lisa Kane

Georgia C. Simpson

Justine Kilkelly Trucksess

ISBN-13: 978-1537151977

ISBN-10: 1537151975

If you would like to write a *Bucket List* about your area,
contact Mary Ann Bolen at MaryAnn.Bolen@gmail.com

Cover photo of Hanover Shoe Farms' Standardbred foal courtesy of Gunjan Patel.

legal disclaimer

This book is designed to provide information, entertainment, and motivation to our readers. It is sold with the understanding that the publisher is not engaged to render any type of physical, psychological, legal, or any other kind of professional advice.

Participation in the activities listed may be dangerous or illegal and could lead to arrest, serious injury, or death.

The content of this book is the sole expression and opinion of its authors and not necessarily that of the publisher. No warranties or guarantees are expressed or implied. This list of experiences is in random sequence.

Neither the publisher nor the individual authors shall be liable for any physical, psychological, emotional, financial, or commercial damages, including, but not limited to, special, incidental, consequential, or other damages.

Our views and rights are the same: You are responsible for your own choices, actions, and results.

The "Detail Squad" photographed at
Guthrie Memorial Library — Hanover's Public Library
(lower step, left to right): Ann E. Diviney and Georgia C. Simpson,
(upper step, left to right): Justine Kilkelly Trucksess and Lisa Kane.

4

dedication

Mary Ann and Bob Bolen were the the instigators of this book. When we purchased their first Ocean City, New Jersey, bucket list book, we thought this would be an easy task, given all that this area provides. Mary Ann and Bob have provided technical guidance and cheered us on. Without these, all our ideas would still be on laptops and small pieces of paper. Thanks, Bolens! We are indebted to you.

We dedicate this book to Richard McAlister, a Scots-Irishman who purchased a tract of land in 1745, built a log home and opened a store and tavern. He divided his farm into lots in 1763 and founded what became Hanover. His choice of land, at the crossing of a road going north from Baltimore and a road going from Philadelphia to Virginia, brought many businesses and immigrants to farm the fertile land. Dedicated workers and owners willing to invest in business production such as cigars, shirts, gloves, silks, flour, power steering gears, shoes, cars, wire cloth, furniture, canned goods, race horses and snack foods helped create a stable population. While some businesses were short-lived, many continue today, allowing the basis for this book.

acknowledgements

Thank you to Jim Simpson, who was the motivator for the book. He is a big idea guy, who left the details of writing the book to others.

A big thanks goes out to those who supplied us with ideas beyond ours that we, the Detail Squad, surgically reduced to the 100 you see here.

Thank you to Guthrie Memorial Library, which provided us a space for creating this book.

Thank you to The Friends of the Guthrie Memorial Library, who have taken on the task for printing and distribution after our job is done.

Special thanks to Robin Fraumeni, who took our ideas, pictures and difficulty with the layout design and turned them into a printable book.

Thanks to Gunjan Patel and Karen Huston for the horse artwork and giving us pictures to chuckle about.

Thanks to Georg R. Sheets, author, historian and associate with York County Library System. Georg attended every meeting, quietly listening to our ideas. When he spoke, it was consequential and positive.

GUTHRIE MEMORIAL LIBRARY
HANOVER'S PUBLIC LIBRARY

FRIENDS OF THE LIBRARY

Proceeds from the sale of this book go to The Friends of the Guthrie Memorial Library—Hanover's Public Library to help sustain and grow library programs.

6

why a bucket list?

Photo courtesy of the Borough of Hanover.

Scores of people descend on neighboring Gettysburg yearly, where there are stories to hear and learn from. Hanover, fourteen miles to the east, also has a rich history. The area is a crossroads with people traveling through, but usually not exploring its unique places. Many residents are tied to the town through their heritage but take for granted that which is here and often miss what our area offers.

Nowadays one can take a virtual reality trip through electronics and not really experience anything. Likewise, one can travel the same route for years and not really see what is present. This book is for first-time visitors and longtime residents to be surprised, find hidden gems not in the travel websites and enjoy those "aha" moments.

Use the checklist in the back as a scavenger game, marking off what you have done. If you do not have much time here or prefer immediate gratification, use the websites listed in this book to help in your search.

Take time to visit the people, not just the locations. That will bring clarity to the following cliche:

> *"Focus on the Journey, not the*
> *destination. Joy is found not in finishing*
> *an activity but in doing it."*
> —*Greg Anderson*

1

sit under a
300-year-old tree

Where??
In back of the Eichelberger Performing Arts Center.

"Someone's sitting in the shade today because someone planted a tree a long time ago."
—*Warren Buffett*

2

what's old and new and read all over?

What??
Guthrie Memorial Library — Hanover's Public Library
merges old world architecture with new world technology.

10

3

tag...you're it!

How??
Play laser tag at Hickory Falls
Family Entertainment Center.

*"Never, ever underestimate the
importance of having fun!"*
—Randy Pausch

4

go fishing

Where??
Lake Marburg and Long Arm Reservoir offer
many species of fish for all skill levels.

5

drive across the Camelback Bridge

Where??
John's Burnt Mill Bridge, a triple-arched stone bridge,
is on the National Register of Historic Places.

6

experience the Gilded Age

How??
Spend an evening at the Sheppard Mansion,
a 1913 Colonial Revival B&B.

7

read "The Adventures of Tom Tiller"

What??

Wirt Barnitz, a 1905 graduate from Eichelberger High School, WWI foreign war correspondent, world traveler and radio commentator, wrote this coming-of-age novel. Find it at Guthrie Memorial Library — Hanover's Public Library.

8

enjoy ale, eats, merriment & live music

Where??
The Circle

*"If more of us valued food and cheer
and song above hoarded gold,
it would be a merrier world."*
—*J.R.R. Tolkien*

9

play 27 holes of golf in one day

How??

South Hills Golf Club is a 27-hole public course
in the rolling hills of south Hanover.

10

see Santa's big entrance into town

When??
A parade the day after Thanksgiving brings
Santa to his cabin, a tradition since 1937.

11

cool off on a dual water slide

Where??
Codorus State Park's swimming pool is one
of the largest pools in Pennsylvania.

12

cheer at a Black Rose Rollers game

How??
Magic Elm Skateland is home to the Hanover women's
flat track roller derby league, founded in 2010.

13

watch out for ghouls, goblins and candy coming at you

When??
Since 1941, the Hanover Area Jaycees
have held the Halloween Parade on Baltimore Street
the last Thursday of October.

21

14

admire a commanding view of Hanover

Where??
The hill at the top of Mt. Olivet Cemetery
is where Union soldiers took their stand to bombard
the Confederates before the Battle of Gettysburg.

15

take a Tiffany stained glass window tour

How??
Check out the spectacular 1920s windows
at St. Matthew Lutheran Church. Visit website.

16

sip a local wine

Why??
The countryside offers splendid views to add to
your pleasure. Ask a local or search online.

*"It's a smile, it's a kiss, it's a sip of wine.
It's summertime!"*
—Kenny Chesney

17

marvel at a flatiron building

What??
This triangular-shaped building is located at York and
Railroad streets and includes a turret and great shopping.

18

locate one of Custer's earliest "stands"

Where??

On the southwest corner of the square, George Custer is said to have tied his horse to a tree during the Battle of Hanover.

19

participate in a living tradition

How??

Buy your fresh produce and meats on Saturday mornings at
the Hanover Market House, in existence since 1815.

20

cruise "The Treat" and use carhop service

Where??
Opened in 1953, Crabbs Tropical Treat on
Route 94 is a local hangout all summer.

21

ride on the Hanover Trolley Trail

How ??
Bike or walk part of the path that was the Hanover Fast Line,
opened in 1908, which ended in York.

22

race a mile in a circle
on tiny wheels

What??
Visit Magic Elm Skateland,
an old-fashioned roller skating rink.

23

get smokin' hot BBQ

How??
Hanover is home to several local BBQ restaurants.
Use your nose to find one.

24

treat your ears to amazing acoustics

Where??
Go to a performance at the Eichelberger
Performing Arts Center, built in 1932.

25

see rare diesel tractors

When??
In May, R.H. Sheppard Museum opens its doors to
celebrate R.H. Sheppard's birthday. Check website.

26

take in a live show

How??

Hanover Little Theatre, located in a former two-room schoolhouse, has held plays with local talent since 1949.

27

attend a Rhinos game

What??

Hanover's semi-pro football team, originally started in 1955 as "sand lotters," plays home games at Manheim Adventure Park.

"There's two times of year for me:
Football season, and waiting for football season."
—*Darius Rucker*

28

stand at the point where local iron ore, soldiers and a president passed through Hanover

Where??
On Railroad Street, find the monument honoring
President Lincoln's quick speech in Hanover
on Nov. 18, 1863, as he traveled to Gettysburg.
Soldiers and iron ore also traveled these rails.

29

choose a winner

When??
Lincoln Speedway, a clay oval track for sprint cars,
has been drawing summer crowds since 1953.

*"Finishing races is important,
but racing is more important."*
—*Dale Earnhardt*

30

two mansions, same floor plan

Why??
C.N. Myers and H.D. Sheppard, business partners
of Hanover Shoe Company, chose to build identical homes
in 1911 and 1913 rather than surpass one another.
Philadelphian Herman Miller was the architect.

31

wolf down a "Famous" gutbuster with everything on it

Where??
The Famous Hot Weiner began in 1923 and still serves up its famous meals, a "must visit" for everyone.

32

go geocaching

How??
Get your Hanover Geo Trail passport
at the Hanover Area Chamber of Commerce.

33

witness a Dock Dog Diving competition

When??
The divers take flight over Lake Marburg
during the Codorus Blast, held in June.

34

play 140 classic arcade games in one day

Where??
Timeline Arcade is the largest arcade in Pennsylvania.

42

35

commune with some rare, 100-year-old trees collected from all over the world

How??
Take time to enjoy the shade under the trees at Myers' Arboretum on Baltimore Street.

36

be lucky enough to see a newborn foal

When??
Racehorse breeding farm Hanover Shoe Farms, the "Greatest Name in Harness Racing," sets foaling season as February to June.

37

discover what 14,341 pipes sound like

How??
Attend a service at St. Matthew Lutheran Church, which owns the eighth largest wind-blown pipe organ in the world.

38

touch history
and a Mason-Dixon
crown stone

Where??
You will find MD60 on Garrett Road off the Baltimore Pike.

39

gorge on
chicken and waffles

How??
Since 1801, The Altland House has been serving
this tradition in Abbottstown, on the Lincoln Highway,
the first U.S. transcontinental highway.

40

get fired up with tons of chili

When??
The Annual Pennsylvania Chili Cook-Off
is Labor Day weekend.

"If you can't stand the heat,
get out of the kitchen."
—President Harry S. Truman

41

conduct an all-volunteer symphony orchestra concert while seated

How??

The Hanover Symphony Orchestra, formed in 1995, performs at the Eichelberger Performing Arts Center.

*"No one can whistle a symphony.
It takes an orchestra to play it."*
—H. E. Luccock

42

snap a selfie with Iron Mike

Where??

Moved from Mt. Olivet Cemetery to the northeast corner of the Hanover Square, Iron Mike, the eternal watchdog, can be found bravely guarding the Picket.

43

view the original magazine story that started a famous opera

What??

Guthrie Memorial Library — Hanover's Public Library contains the 1898 *Century Magazine* story by Hanover's John Luther Long, which was the basis of *Madame Butterfly*.

44

rate a new
flavor of pretzel

How??
Visit the factory outlet store of Snyder's of Hanover,
founded in 1909 as a bakery in Hanover by Harry Warehime.

45

study a priceless
old cookbook with
18th-century recipes

Where??
Built in 1783, the Neas House was home to many
outstanding Hanover citizens. Restored by the Hanover Area
Historical Society, it houses many treasures from long ago.

46

be a localvore

Why??
Treat yourself and buy the best locally produced
beef, pork, produce and gifts at Carriage House Market.

47

find thousands of shoes in a basement

When??
In September and May, the Clarks Shoe Outlet
on Center Square has bargains galore in the basement.

48

eat 'til you can't stuff anymore in

Where??
Attend a fire hall oyster feed.

*"People who love to eat
are always the best people."*
—*Julia Child*

49

walk among the last earthly addresses of 1,400 soldiers

How??
Mt. Olivet Cemetery has soldiers buried from
every war since the Revolutionary War.

50

stand at the intersection of Irishtown Road and Irishtown Road

Why??
Find where New Oxford and Hanover meet.

*"The person attempting to travel
two roads at once will get nowhere."*
—Xun Zi

51

sing from 100-year-old carol booklets

When??
Emmanuel UCC church shares its songs
and carol booklets, donated from John Wanamaker
himself, the Sunday before Christmas.

52

walk amidst 3,000 American flags

Where??
The Exchange Club of Hanover's 9/11
Memorial Healing Field® display is held every few
years at rotating locations. Check website.

53

find inspiration with local poets and musicians

How??
Ask around to learn where these loyal bards
meet for open mic nights or poetry readings.

54

spot the local caged lion

Why??
In 1906, architect Herman Miller of Philadelphia
entrusted this beast to protect the Hanover Saving Fund
Society on Carlisle Street. The name and doorway
have changed, but the feline remains.

55

discover a
different set of tools

What??
The Pennsylvania Room at Guthrie Memorial Library —
Hanover's Public Library contains records and
lists any genealogist would treasure.

"History remembers only the celebrated,
genealogy remembers them all."
— Laurence Overmire

56

buy an
original treasure

Where??
Art Downtown contains many
talented local artists' originals.

57

check out the steps taken to get chips freshly made and delivered to your grocery

How??
Visit the Utz Quality Foods factory tour and outlet store.

58

bring the dead to life

Why??
Visit with Friends of Mt. Olivet Cemetery who,
through the Garden of Souls project, are "digging" to find
what the dead would tell us with historic tales.

59

liberate a "European" village

When??
In New Oxford each September,
80 World War II vehicles and 400 re-enactors "liberate"
the town and honor remaining veterans from that war.

60

feel the mist rising
from the dam as you
attend an Easter
sunrise service

How??
St. Bartholomew's United Church welcomes
all for the service at Long Arm Dam.

61

monkey around,
cross a high bridge,
climb a castle tower

Where??
Kids Kingdom Playground is in Penn Township.

62

devour a
hand-twisted original
sourdough pretzel

Why??

Revonah* has been the best place for this specialty since 1935.

Revonah is Hanover spelled backwards.

63

drink a local brew

How??

Hanover has several local microbreweries.
Ask a native where to find them.

64

find a ghost

How??
Roam the halls of the Eichelberger Professional Building,
built as a boys academy in 1896 by Captain Abdiel W. Eichelberger
(1819-1901). Many have felt his presence.

65

savor the grounds of the oldest stone Roman Catholic church in the U.S.

Why??

Conewago Chapel, originally a log-dwelling chapel built in 1741, was completed in 1787 with stone walls and a beautiful location. It is also called Basilica of the Sacred Heart of Jesus.

66

dine on crab cakes and an orange crush

Where??

Bay City, the oldest seafood restaurant in Hanover, was started by Ted Smith from the back of his Volkswagen bug.

67

cheer a 75-year rivalry from the stands

What??
Watch the Hanover High School versus Delone Catholic football game. Husbands and wives have been known to talk trash and sit on opposite sides of the stadium to root for their respective alma maters.

68

walk the
City of the Dead

How??

Mt. Olivet Cemetery, once known by that name,
is home to 14,000 — with space still available for you.

69

catch up on the news

Where??
Culp's Hanover News Agency, in business since 1923,
is located on the site of McAlister's Tavern, where
Ben Franklin was a guest in 1755.

*"We're a newsstand and we also hear
the news." — Will Rickrode*

70

view the newly restored Gettysburg Electric Map

When??
The Hanover Heritage and Conference Center
has map programs Thursday-Saturday on the second floor.
Check website.

71

catch a glimpse of an underwater ghost town

How??

When water levels are low in Lake Marburg, rooftops, roads and foundations can be seen of the flooded town of Marburg.

72

breakfast on home fries and scrapple

Where??
The Little Red Schoolhouse, built in 1894 as the Locust
Grove School, serves up great traditional breakfasts.

73

celebrate Pennsylvania Dutch heritage

When??

Held the last Saturday in July, Dutch Days began in 1984 to celebrate the culture of Hanover's German immigrants, who arrived in the late 1700s.

74

try coffee off
the beaten path

Where??
Merlin's roasts and brews fine coffee and boasts of
daily coffee specials from around the world.

*"Coffee, the finest organic
suspension ever devised."*
— *Star Trek: Voyager*

75

delight in eating a raspberry soft-serve ice cream cone

Where??
Try the specialty of York Street Treat.

*"Life is like an ice cream,
enjoy it before it melts."*
— Unknown

76

hunt for 63 holes using only a plastic disc

Where??

Codorus State Park contains three PDGA courses of disc golf, a fast and inexpensive alternative to golf.

77

stretch out on the grass and open your ears to live music

When??
In the summer months, every Sunday at the
Codorus Band Shell and once a month at the Warehime-Myers
Mansion, lively music is enjoyed by all who attend.

78

learn how far a Civil War artillery shell can travel through walls

How??
Follow the Battle of Hanover Walking Tour to the
Winebrenner House and read the *Wayside* for the answer.

79

go to a mansion
to hunt for 3D ovals

When??
At Easter, the Hanover Area Historical Society hosts
the egg hunt at the Warehime-Myers Mansion.

80

relish a rarity

What??
Reader's Café is an independent bookstore.

*"Let us read, and let us dance;
these two amusements will never
do any harm to the world."*
— Voltaire

81

commune with nature, walk among sculptures

Where??
Starr Pottery and Bronze Sculpture and Nature Trail.

*"The key to understanding any people
is in its art; its writing, painting, sculpture."*
—*Louis L'Amour*

82

tiny house movement — Hanover-style

What??
Check out the miniature houses,
all in a row, on Green Springs Road.

83

join in an event that cost 25 cents in 1893 and continues today

Why??
The Conewago Chapel Picnic serves up food and fun
in July for a good cause. The cost has increased.

84

discover the connection among shoes, racehorses, a newspaper and a hospital

What??

Two men, C.N. Myers and H.D. Sheppard, founded Hanover Shoe Co. (now Clarks), Hanover Shoe Farms, *The Evening Sun* of Hanover and Hanover Hospital. All businesses are still here.

85

splurge at Hanover's only deli

Where??
Locally owned Shultz's Deli has been serving
quality, homemade food since 1939.

86

check out the chalk

How??
In June, artists with Chalk it Up Hanover take to the
sidewalks to create temporary masterpieces.

87

be on a boat for a blast

Why??

During the Codorus Blast Festival in the Park, spectacular night fireworks over the lake are viewed best on the water.

88

listen to old-time Pennsylvania Dutch hymn singing

When??
Historic mid-19th-century Wildasin Meeting House holds an annual Brethren service at 2 p.m. the first Sunday in June.

89

the ground that two Hanover Shoe Farms barns rest on has a story to tell

What??

When visiting the main farm, imagine how much dirt it took to build the barns up onto high ground. The dirt hole became a swimming pool that ended up larger than Olympic-size.

90

find safety in candy, chainsaws, costumes and cider

Where??
Halloween in the Park, started in 2008 at Codorus State Park,
provides a safe place to enjoy season festivities.

91

take a trip down memory lane

How??
See an original Hanover Car at the
Hanover Museum near New Oxford.

92

track down
literary canines

Where??
Guthrie Memorial Library — Hanover's Public Library
hosts Reading Therapy Dogs several times a month.

*"Happiness is a warm puppy
and a good book."*
— Charles M. Schultz,
originator of Peanuts cartoon

93

sound an alarm

How??
Visit the Hanover Fire Department Museum,
where 200 years of firefighting is preserved.

94

guess how many miles of fence Hanover Shoe Farms maintains

How many??

☐ 85   ☐ 135   ☐ 195   ☐ 265

(the answer is on the brochure at the farm)

95

float your boat

Where??
Kayak on Lake Marburg.

"Everyone must believe in something.
I believe I'll go kayaking.
— anonymous

96

choose hard or soft — crabs

Where??
Seafood is served with a smile at Big Mike's Crabhouse.

97

admire beauty designed by a comic strip artist

What??

Raymond Perry, artist for Batman and other comics, designed
Guthrie Memorial Library's large stained glass window.

98

listen to the story told by rocks

How??
Drive through the Pigeon Hills with the
Chamber of Commerce guide to see remnants
of Precambrian volcanoes and more.

99

celebrate a patriotic event that started here in 1868

What??

Salute the town's veterans in the annual Memorial Day parade.

100

sight flight
through a lens

What??
View the Codorus bald eagle and osprey nests
safely with binoculars from land or water.

i did it

- [ ] 1. sit under a 300-year-old tree
- [ ] 2. what's old and new and read all over?
- [ ] 3. tag...you're it!
- [ ] 4. go fishing
- [ ] 5. drive across the Camelback Bridge
- [ ] 6. experience the Gilded Age
- [ ] 7. read "The Adventures of Tom Tiller"
- [ ] 8. enjoy ale, eats, merriment & live music
- [ ] 9. play 27 holes of golf in one day
- [ ] 10. see Santa's big entrance into town
- [ ] 11. cool off in a dual water slide
- [ ] 12. cheer at a Black Rose Rollers game
- [ ] 13. watch out for ghouls, goblins and candy coming at you
- [ ] 14. admire a commanding view of Hanover
- [ ] 15. take a Tiffany stained glass window tour
- [ ] 16. sip a local wine

☐ 17. marvel at a flatiron building

☐ 18. locate one of Custer's earliest "stands"

☐ 19. participate in a living tradition

☐ 20. cruise "The Treat" and use carhop service

☐ 21. ride on the Hanover Trolley Trail

☐ 22. race a mile in a circle on tiny wheels

☐ 23. get smokin' hot BBQ

☐ 24. treat your ears to amazing acoustics

☐ 25. see rare diesel tractors

☐ 26. take in a live show

☐ 27. attend a Rhinos game

☐ 28. stand at the point where local iron ore, soldiers and a president passed through Hanover

☐ 29. choose a winner

☐ 30. two mansions, same floor plan

☐ 31. wolf down a "Famous" gutbuster with everything on it

☐ 32. go geocaching

☐ 33. witness a Dock Dog Diving competition

☐ 34. play 140 classic arcade games in one day

☐ 35. commune with some rare, 100-year-old trees collected from all over the world

☐ 36. be lucky enough to see a newborn foal

☐ 37. discover what 14,341 pipes sound like

☐ 38. touch history and a Mason-Dixon crown stone

☐ 39. gorge on chicken and waffles

☐ 40. get fired up with tons of chili

☐ 41. conduct an all-volunteer symphony orchestra concert while seated

☐ 42. snap a selfie with Iron Mike

☐ 43. view the original magazine story that started a famous opera

☐ 44. rate a new flavor of pretzel

☐ 45. study a priceless old cookbook with 18th-century recipes

☐ 46. be a localvore

☐ 47. find thousands of shoes in a basement

☐ 48. eat 'til you can't stuff anymore in

☐ 49. walk among the last earthly addresses of 1,400 soldiers

☐ 50. stand at the intersection of Irishtown Road and Irishtown Road

☐ 51. sing from 100-year-old carol booklets

☐ 52. walk amidst 3,000 American flags

☐ 53. find inspiration with local poets and musicians

☐ 54. spot the local caged lion

☐ 55. discover a different set of tools

☐ 56. buy an original treasure

☐ 57. check out the steps taken to get chips freshly made and delivered to your grocery

☐ 58. bring the dead to life

☐ 59. liberate a "European" village

☐ 60. feel the mist rising from the dam as you attend an Easter sunrise service

☐ 61. monkey around, cross a high bridge, climb a castle tower

☐ 62. devour a hand-twisted original sourdough pretzel

☐ 63. drink a local brew

☐ 64. find a ghost

☐ 65. savor the grounds of the oldest stone Roman Catholic church in the U. S.

☐ 66. dine on crab cakes and an orange crush

☐ 67. cheer a 75-year rivalry from the stands

☐ 68. walk the City of the Dead

☐ 69. catch up on the news

☐ 70. view the newly restored Gettysburg Electric Map

☐ 71. catch a glimpse of an underwater ghost town

☐ 72. breakfast on home fries and scrapple

☐ 73. celebrate Pennsylvania Dutch heritage

☐ 74. try coffee off the beaten path

☐ 75. delight in eating a raspberry soft-serve ice cream cone

☐ 76. hunt for 63 holes using only a plastic disc

☐ 77. stretch out on the grass and open your ears to live music

☐ 78. learn how far a Civil War artillery shell can travel through walls

☐ 79. go to a mansion to hunt for 3D ovals

☐ 80. relish a rarity

☐ 81. commune with nature, walk among sculptures

☐ 82. tiny house movement — Hanover-style

☐ 83. join in an event that cost 25 cents in 1893 and continues today

☐ 84. discover the connection among shoes, racehorses, a newspaper and a hospital

☐ 85. splurge at Hanover's only deli

☐ 86. check out the chalk

☐ 87. be on a boat for a blast

☐ 88. listen to old-time Pennsylvania Dutch hymn singing

☐ 89. the ground that two Hanover Shoe Farms barns rest on has a story to tell

☐ 90. find safety in candy, chainsaws, costumes and cider

☐ 91. take a trip down memory lane

☐ 92. track down literary canines

The Warehime-Myers Mansion at 305 Baltimore Street in Hanover is home of the Hanover Area Historical Society.

☐ 93. sound an alarm

☐ 94. guess how many miles of fence Hanover Shoe Farms maintains

☐ 95. float your boat

☐ 96. choose hard or soft — crabs

☐ 97. admire beauty designed by a comic strip artist

☐ 98. listen to the story told by rocks

☐ 99. celebrate a patriotic event that started here in 1868

☐ 100. sight flight through a lens

about the authors

Ann E. Diviney is a writer and poet living in Adams County, Pennsylvania. She spent 25 years as a columnist, features writer and features editor with *The Evening Sun* in Hanover. She has been published in *The Philadelphia Inquirer*, *The Pittsburgh Post-Gazette*, *The Harrisburg Patriot News*, *Central PA Magazine*, *Keystone Conservationist*, *Mid-Atlantic Country* and *Country Accents*, among others. She is the author of *From Sea to Shining Sea: A Hike Across America on Old U.S. 30*.

"With thoughts of my parents, Jake Diviney and the late Ann Spangler Diviney, both of whom grew up in Hanover and graduated from Eichelberger High School, Class of '46. Even though they probably weren't conceived under The Picket, and did not have three generations in the ground here, I will always think of them as Hanoverians".

Lisa Kane grew up in Riviera Beach, Maryland, and currently resides in Hanover, Pennsylvania, with her husband, three sons and dog, Dixie. She holds a Master's Degree in Library Science from The University of Pittsburgh, a Bachelor's Degree in Education from Towson University and an Associate's Degree from Anne Arundel Community College. Lisa is the Executive Director of Guthrie Memorial Library in Hanover. She enjoys reading and spending time with her family at the beach.

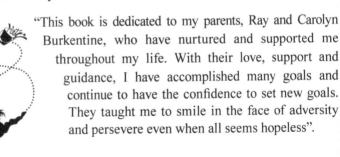

"This book is dedicated to my parents, Ray and Carolyn Burkentine, who have nurtured and supported me throughout my life. With their love, support and guidance, I have accomplished many goals and continue to have the confidence to set new goals. They taught me to smile in the face of adversity and persevere even when all seems hopeless".

Georgia C. Simpson moved to the Hanover area in 1992 due to her husband's career move. Impressed by the strong family values and work ethic and extensive list of products produced in the area, she marveled in discoveries down every street and alley, where private businesses, old cemeteries, historic markers and well-groomed homes abound. Although not a writer by profession, Georgia seized the opportunity to use this book format to share local treasures with the world. Georgia's favorite treasure: the people of Hanover, including Ann, Lisa and Justine, the other members of the "Detail Squad."

"This book is dedicated to my husband, best friend and confidant, Jim Simpson, whose optimism through the years convinced me I could do strange things like start my own business, drive a large tractor, take flying lessons and write this book."

Justine Kilkelly Trucksess is a newcomer to the world of book writing, but she is no stranger to Downtown Hanover! Justine works as the Manager of Main Street Hanover, the local downtown revitalization effort. Growing up an Army Brat, and never one to stand still, Justine has lived in many places near and far, but she has chosen to make Hanover her home.

"I would like to dedicate this book to my wonderfully supportive husband, Andrew, for allowing me to follow my passion where it leads; my son Xavier, and my loving parents, Frank and Ann Kilkelly for moving our family to Hanover in 2001. I would also like to thank the downtown Hanover business owners for being so unique and making my job so special and the Hanover Area Chamber of Commerce staff for helping to brainstorm 100+ bucket list ideas that make our hometown so wonderful."

books in the
bucket list series:

The Hanover, Pennsylvania, Bucket List,
    by Ann E. Diviney, Lisa Kane, Georgia C. Simpson
    and Justine Kilkelly Trucksess

The Havana Bucket List, by David Sloan and Rob O'Neal

The Kentucky Bucket List, by Michael Crisp

The Key West Bucket List, by David Sloan

The Newburyport, Massachusetts Bucket List,
    by Chris Johnston, Sheila Bridgland, and Jessamyn Anderson

The Ocean City Bucket List, by Mary Ann Bolen

The Ohio Bucket List, by Michael Crisp

The Pittsburgh, Pennsylvania Bucket List,
    by Susan B. Malcolm, Ph.D.

The Tennessee Bucket List, by Michael Crisp

The Wisconsin Bucket List, by Kelly Jo Stull

Sculpted by Cyrus Dallin and dedicated in 1904, "The Picket"
monument was placed on Hanover's Center Square to honor the Union
Cavalry who fought during the Battle of Hanover (June 30, 1863).
According to local legend, the dog "Iron Mike" previously resided
at Hanover's Mt. Olivet Cemetery until he began scaring horses.

Websites & Phone Numbers

For your immediate information or gratification, these websites and phone numbers are provided and are valid as of date of publication. We offer no guarantees for future information accuracy. Numbers with an asterisk, but no information, offer you a challenge and a degree of satisfaction when you find them. If you get stumped, contact Guthrie Memorial Library at 717-632-5183 or the Chamber of Commerce at 717-637-6130.

1. www.theeich.org
   717-637-7086

2. www.yorklibraries.org/guthrie
   717-632-5183

3. www.hickoryfalls.com
   717-632-9907

4. www.stateparks.com/codorus.html
   717-637-2816, 888-727-2757

5. http://bridgehunter.com/
   pa/adams/17216042830560

6. www.sheppardmansion.com
   717-633-8075

7. www.yorklibraries.org/guthrie
   717-632-5183

8. www.thecirclehanoverpa.com
   717-637-0000

9. www.southhillsgc.com
   717-637-7500

10. www.hanoverpasantacabin.com

11. www.stateparks.com/codorus.html
    717-637-2816, 888-727-2757

12. www.blackroserollers.com
    717-632-1888
    (*Magic Elm Skateland*)

13. www.facebook.com/
    hanoverhalloweenparade

14. www.mtolivetcemetery
    association.org
    717-637-5294

15. www.stmattlutheran.org/
    about-us/history/
    stained-glass-window-tour
    717-637-7101

16. http://m.pennsylvaniawine.com/
    wine_trail/2-mason-dixon-
    wine-trail

17. www.facebook.com/
    treasures.hanover
    717-637-8408

18. http://explorepahistory.com/
    attraction.php?id=1-B-3886

19. www.hanover-market.com
    717-632-1353

20. https://www.facebook.com/
    pages/Crabbs-Tropical-Treat/
    386124854792700
    717-632-3977

21. www.traillink.com

22. www.magicelmskateland.com
717-632-1888

23. *

24. www.theeich.org
717-637-7086

25. www.rhsheppard.com
717-637-3751

26. www.hanoverlittletheatre.com
717-637-5297

27. www.hanoverrhinos.org
717-465-0782

28. *

29. www.lincolnspeedway.com
717-624-2755

30. http://hahs.us/mansion
717-632-3207, 717-637-6413

    www.sheppardmansion.com
    717-633-8075

31. www.famoushotweiner.com
717-637-1282

32. www.hanoverchamber.com/
visitors/hanover-geo-trail
717-637-6130

33. www.dockdogs.com

34. www.timelinearcade.net
717-634-2600

35. http://hahs.us/mansion
717-632-3207, 717-637-6413

36. www.hanoverpa.com
717-637-8931

37. www.stmattlutheran.org
717-637-7101

38. www.hahs.us/markers.html

39. altlandhouse.com
717-259-9535

40. www.hanoverchilicookoff.com

41. www.hanoversymphony
orchestra.org
717-632-8067

42. http://www.yorkblog.com/
yorktownsquare/2006/2/13/
iron-mike-guards-the-picket

43. www.yorklibraries.org/guthrie
717-632-5183

44. www.snydersofhanover.com
800-233-7125, ext. 28592 for tours

45. www.hahs.us/neas.html
717-632-3207

46. www.facebook.com/
thecarriagehousemarket
717-633-7500

47. www.clarksusa.com
717-637-9157

48 *

49. www.mtolivetcemetery
association.org
717-637-5294

50. https://www.google.com/
?gws_rd=ssl#q=intersection
+of+irishtown+road+and
+irishtown+road+and+
new+oxford+and+hanover

51. www.emmanuelucc.org
717-632-8281

52. www.hanoverexchangeclub.com
or www.healingfield.org/
hanover16 *(change the number
according to the year)*

53. *

54. www.visualrealia.com
/articles/2016/7/16/
hanovers-caged-lion
717-632-9711

55. www.yorklibraries.org/
guthrie-pa-room
717-632-5183

56. www.hanoverareaarts.com
717-632-2521

57. www.utzsnacks.com/
utz-factory.html
800-367-7629

58. www.friendsofmtolivet
cemetery.org
717-637-5294

59. www.liberationofnewoxford.com
717-338-9114

60. www.stbart-hanoverpa.org/
Prod/JoinUs/dsp_service_
detail.cfm
717-632-1952

61. www.penntwp.com/
Parks---Recreation.html
717-632-7366

62. www.revonahpretzel.com
717-630-2883

63. www.pennlive.com/
entertainment/index.
ssf/2015/08/hanover_a_craft_
beer_destinati.html

64. www.theeich.org/history
717-637-7086

65. www.sacredheartbasilica.com
717-637-2721

66. www.baycityrestaurant.com
717-637-1217

67. www.gametimepa.com or
www.maxpreps.com

68. www.mtolivetcemetery
association.org
717-637-5294

69. www.mainstreethanover.org/
explore/details/hanover-
news-agency-culps
717-637-5208

70. www.hanoverhcc.com
717-739-8364

71. http://www.hereayear.com/
underwater-ghost-town-
now-a-pa-playground

http://www.dcnr.state.pa.us/
stateparks/findapark/codorus
717-637-2816, 888-727-2757

72. www.littleredschoolrestaurant.com
717-688-6308

73. www.hanoverchamber.com/
dutch-festival
717-637-6130

74. https://www.yelp.com/biz/
merlins-coffee-hanover
717-632-7692

75. https://www.yelp.com/biz/
york-street-treat-hanover
717-637-4165

76. https://www.discgolfscene.com/
courses/Codorus_State_Park
717-637-2816
888-727-2757

77. www.hahs.us/mansion
717-637-6413
http://www.dcnr.state.pa.us/
stateparks/findapark/codorus/
717-637-2816
888-727-2757

78. www.hanoverchamber.com/
wp-content/uploads/2014/10/
NewrevisedBOHbrochure_
web.pdf
717-637-6130

79. www.hahs.us/mansion
717-637-6413

80. www.thereaderscafe.net
717-630-2524

81. www.starrpottery.com
717-632-0027

82. *

83. sacredheartbasilica.com/
events/parish-picnic
717-637-2721

84. *

85. www.shultzsdeli.com
717-632-9190

86. www.mainstreethanover.org
717-637-6130

87. www.codorusblast.org
717-637-2816

88. 717-637-2816
888-727-2757

89. www.hanoverpa.com
717-637-8931

90. www.halloweeninthepark.org
717-451-3635

91. www.facebook.com/
hanovermuseum
717-476-1183

92. www.yorklibraries.org/guthrie
717-632-5183

93. www.hanoverfiremuseum.com
717-637-6671

94. www.hanoverpa.com
717-637-8931

95. www.dcnr.state.pa.us
717-637-2816

96. www.bigmikescrabhouse.com
717-632-1733

97. www.yorklibraries.org/guthrie
717-632-5183

98. www.hanoverchamber.com
717-637-6130

99. www.hanoverkiwanis.org

100. www.dcnr.state.pa.us
717-637-2816